INTRODUCTION

When you hand-make a quilt, you interact with every single piece of fabric—again and again! This special process lets you build a personal connection with the materials, helping you notice their textures, colors, and patterns in a whole new light. Over time, your quilt transforms into a beloved companion.

Hand-sewn quilts have a charm and warmth that's simply unmatched. They're soft, cuddly, and feel like lifelong friends, even when they're freshly stitched.

English paper-piecing (EPP) is a timeless quilting technique that dates back to the 1770s—and it's wonderfully simple to learn! Here's how it works:

You start with stiff paper templates that fit together like a puzzle, using either one repeating shape or a mix of different ones. Fabric is cut slightly larger than the paper, leaving a generous ¼" seam allowance. The fabric is then wrapped around the paper and secured with thread or glue basting. Once your pieces are ready, you stitch them together to create beautiful quilt blocks.

I used the EPP blocks in this book in my quilt, *Embracing Adventure*. Instructions on making this complete quilt are in *Hand Sewing* (C&T Publishing).

HANDY POCKET GUIDE

ENGLISH PAPER PIECING

Becky Goldsmith

Everything to Get You Started
8 EPP Blocks

Contents

SUPPLIES

English Paper-Piecing Specialty Paper (by C&T Publishing) or smooth white 60- to 65-pound card stock: 18 sheets 8½″ × 11″ for EPP blocks and border flowers—plus a few extra sheets in case of mistakes

Fabric glue pen with disappearing glue: I like the Select Fabric Glue Stick by Quilters Select with the bright yellow glue.

Apliquick Rods (optional)

Basting thread: This thread needs to be strong and light in color. Just about any 28- to 40-weight thread will work. (I use King Tut by Superior Threads or Aurifil's 28-weight cotton.)

EPP thread: The key to less visible stitches is to choose fine 2-ply, 50- to 80-weight thread in colors that match the fabric. When choosing between 2 different colors, try the lighter color/value first. I use either Aurifil 80-weight cotton or Superior's Masterpiece 50-weight 2-ply thread that is available on prewound bobbins.

Basting Needle: A stout needle works best. I prefer the #9 Crewel by Bohin

Sewing Needles: Any needle can work, but you might find it easier to sew with a medium-size needle. Needles that are too sharp/fine burrow into the paper. A bigger needle skims the edge of the papers better. I like the #9 Piecing Needle by Tulip. A milliners needle (such as #11 Milliners Needle by Sue Daley Designs), #10 embroidery needle, or a #10 sharps are good choices.

Thimbles: Thimbles can get in the way when hand sewing, but if your fingers get sore, an adhesive leather thimble pad saves the day. I sometimes use an open-ended ring or tailor's thimble for EPP.

Mini Wonder Clips: These useful clips hold EPP shapes together without distortion.

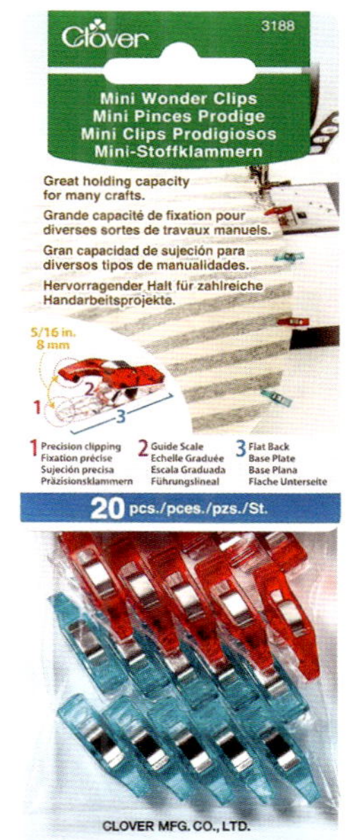

GENERAL INSTRUCTIONS

FABRIC PREPARATION

A few notes about fabric preparation:

- Cotton fabric shrinks, and you can't tell by look or feel how much an individual fabric might shrink. Fabric can be stretched during the manufacturing process, so sometimes just getting fabric wet or steaming it with an iron can cause it to shrink.
- Fabric dyes can bleed when wet. Water chemistry, which varies from place to place, has an impact on dye migration.
- Fabric off the bolt has been treated with a wide array of chemicals that cause allergic reactions in some people.

I always wash my fabric in the washer and dry it in the dryer before using it to remove excess dyes and chemicals and to shrink it to its final size. I don't add any "spray" products to fabrics before I use them. I use a steam iron as needed. I like the feel of washed fabric and find it easier to work with.

It has become commonplace to use fabric straight from bolt. If that is your choice, you won't be alone. But please be aware that when you wash your finished quilt, you may run into problems.

When washing fabric or a quilt, use a neutral detergent without added softeners. All Free and Clear, Retro Wash, and Orvus Paste are good choices. Add ColorCatchers (by Shout), Retayne, and/or Synthrapol to deal with dye migration.

KNOTS

These are the simple and secure knots I use to begin and end my stitching.

Beginning Knot

1. Hold the eye end of a threaded needle between the thumb and index finger of your left or right hand.

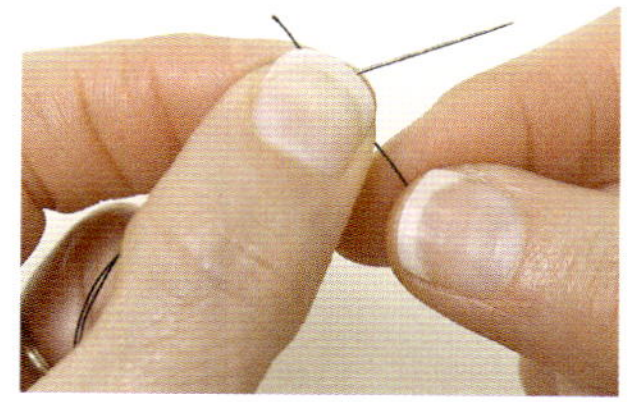

2. Bring the long end of the thread up to and behind the needle with your other hand. Leave ⅜″–½″ tail of thread above the needle. The knot forms where the thread crosses the needle.

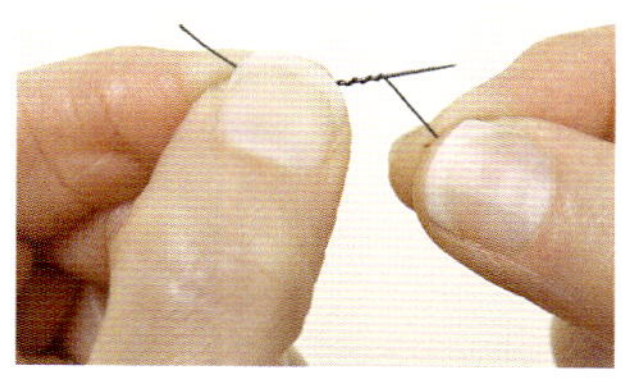

3. Pinch the thread to the needle and wrap the thread 3–5 times around the needle. Finer thread requires more wraps.

4. Pull the wraps down the shaft of the needle until you can pinch them between your thumb and index finger. *If you can see any of the thread wraps, your knot will fall apart as you pull the needle through.*

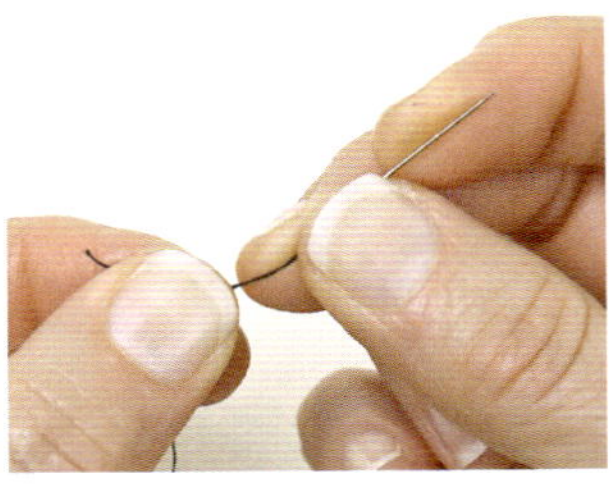

5. Gently pull the needle from between your pinched fingers. Hold onto the thread wraps until the knot forms.

EPP Ending Knot

1. When you are ready to end a line of stitches, take a small backstitch, leaving a loop of thread.

2. Send the needle through the loop and pull it tight. Once is usually enough, but you can make a second knot if you like.

3. Run the needle through a nearby seam allowance to bury the tail of thread. Cut the thread.

SEAM ALLOWANCES FOR EPP

I recommend a "healthy" ¼" seam allowance for EPP. A healthy ¼" seam allowance is bigger than ¼" but not as big as ⅜". It is almost—but not quite—5⁄16" wide, as shown at right.

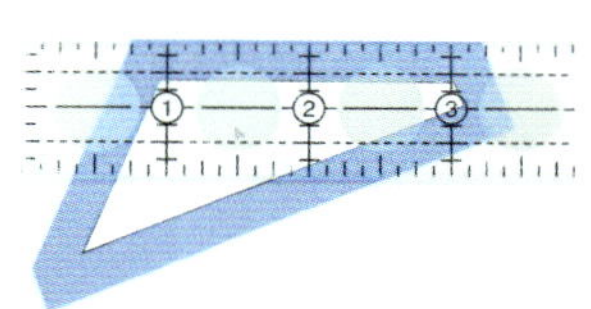

Here's why you need a bigger seam allowance:

* In EPP, the paper takes up space in the fold, which reduces the size of the seam allowance.
* The EPP stitch takes a bigger bite out of the edge of the fabric than a straight stitch does.
* Raw edges fray when you remove papers, especially those that have been glue basted.
* Raw edges fray with handling. This is true when you hand piece small shapes and as you set the quilt together.

As you finish sewing shapes together, you may decide that your seam allowances are overly large. It's okay to very carefully trim them, as long as you keep future frayed edges in mind.

ENGLISH PAPER-PIECING TECHNIQUES

English paper-piecing (EPP) is not new. The technique dates to the 1770s and is very easy to master. Here's how it works:

You begin with stiff paper shapes that fit together like a puzzle. In some cases, one shape is repeated, and the color and value of the fabrics change to make a design. Squares, diamonds, and hexagons are good examples of this. More complex patterns contain a variety of different shapes that fit together to make stars, wheels, and more.

Fabric is cut to fit each paper shape, plus a healthy ¼" seam allowance. The fabric is wrapped around the paper, and the seam allowance is thread or glue basted to the back of the paper. The fabric-covered shapes are then stitched together to make the block.

PREPARE THE PATTERNS

The patterns in the book are a portion of the pattern. Copy the page the specified number of times. You can also download and print the patterns in larger sections. Use the QR code below or go to this address for the downloadable and printable patterns:
tinyurl.com/20557-patterns-download

* TIP *

DIY Patterns

There are many different shapes and sizes of precut papers, but some blocks (like the ones in this book) contain unique shapes. As I designed these blocks, I realized that the design possibilities are endless.

If I can design EPP blocks, you can too! Start with a finished size outline of your block and fill the space with your design. Pay attention to the way the shapes fit together. Your block can be quick to sew with big pieces or complex with harder-to-sew shapes. The choice is yours.

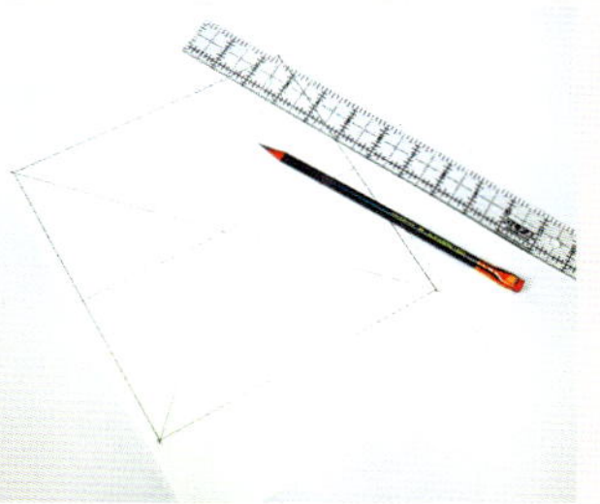

PREPARE THE PAPERS

This book contains 8 different 8″ × 8″ EPP block patterns (see The Blocks, pages 29–45) that you can mix and match in a variety of ways.

Each shape in a pattern is numbered to indicate its placement. When you copy or print the blocks onto EPP paper, these numbers will be on the back side of the papers so you can refer to them as you make your blocks. The blank side of the papers corresponds to the right side of the fabric.

Block 1 is the only directional block. The triangular "flags" will point to the right in the finished block.

✻ TIP ✻

You Are in Control

You hold the scissors, which means you control the paper shapes. If you want to combine small contiguous shapes into a larger shape, do it! The corner triangles offer a good example.

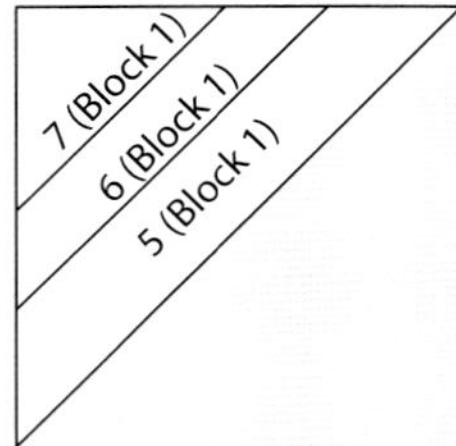

The corners contain three shapes. I strongly recommend that you set aside the uncut block corners until your block centers are complete.

When the time came for me to choose fabric, I realized that my blocks looked better with only two corner fabrics, so I combined the two outer shapes.

There are similar opportunities to combine shapes in most blocks.

1. Copy or print the pattern page onto EPP paper or white card stock. Colored card stock can shadow through your fabric, which is a problem on the design wall.

2. Trim away the excess paper from around the square. Always cut down the center of the lines—*do not cut to the outside or inside of the solid lines.*

3. Cut the block apart on the solid lines. Clip the shapes together by number. Keep the shapes for each block together.

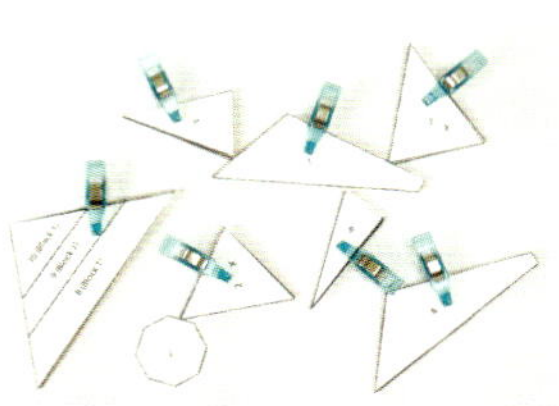

4. Do not cut the 3 strips in the corners apart at this time. Set them aside until it is time to choose the corner fabric(s).

FABRIC-CUTTING INSTRUCTIONS

There are opportunities to fussy cut your fabric in every block. Stripes, plaids, and other directional prints, as well as prints with interesting motifs, are loads of fun to use!

Use a hinged mirror to audition fabric for fussy cutting.

1. Press your fabric to remove wrinkles and creases.

2. Turn the fabric wrong side up on a rotary cutting mat.

3. Use a tiny dab of fabric glue on the blank side of a paper piece to hold it in place on the fabric.

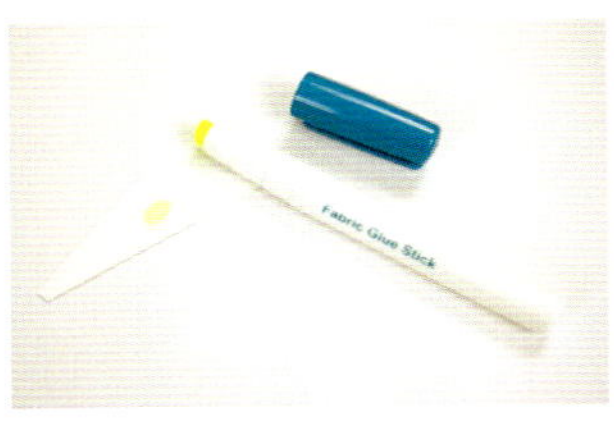

4. Place the paper piece, printed side up, on the fabric. Position it as desired for fussy cutting.

5. Carefully cut the fabric around the paper, leaving a healthy ¼″ seam allowance all the way around the shape (see Seam Allowances for EPP, page 11). Use either scissors or a rotary cutter and ruler—whichever works better for the shapes you are cutting.

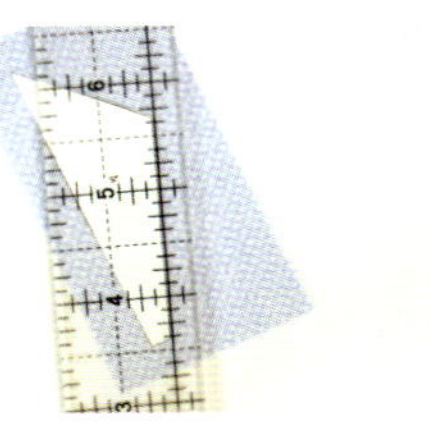

6. If you place more than one shape on the fabric, be sure to leave at least ⅝″ between the paper shapes.

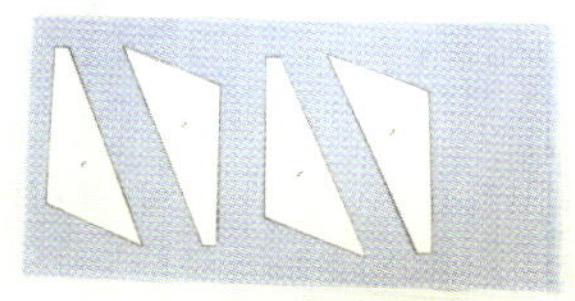

BASTING

Seam allowances can be basted to the shape with thread or fabric glue. Thread basting is slower, but the paper is easier to remove later. Glue basting is faster, but the fabric is prone to fraying when you remove the papers.

I use both methods depending on my mood and the size and shape of the paper piece. Surprisingly, it is easier to thread baste small, sharp shapes.

Thread Basting

Use a stout needle (see Basting Needles, page 6). I like the #9 Crewel Needle by Bohin paired with a strong 28- to 40-weight thread in a light color to avoid dye transfer. I use Aurifil's 28-weight cotton thread (see Thread, page 6).

1. Fold the seam allowance over the edges of the paper. Do not pull the seam allowances too tightly over the paper. Sew through the seam allowance, paper, and fabric on the front of the shape.

2. Your next stitch will be front to back, through the paper, catching the seam allowance. There's no need to make tiny basting stitches—take only as many as you need to hold the seam allowances in place.

3. Repeat for all sides of the shape. Leave the seam allowance at points free so you can move it out of the way as you sew.

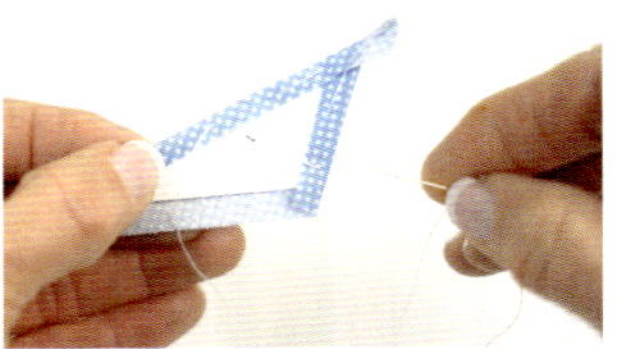

Glue Basting

Choose a fabric glue that dries clear. I use the glue pen with bright yellow glue by Quilters Select.

1. Place the trimmed paper/fabric shape on a firm surface, paper side up.

2. Run a light line of glue about ⅛" away from the cut edge of the paper.

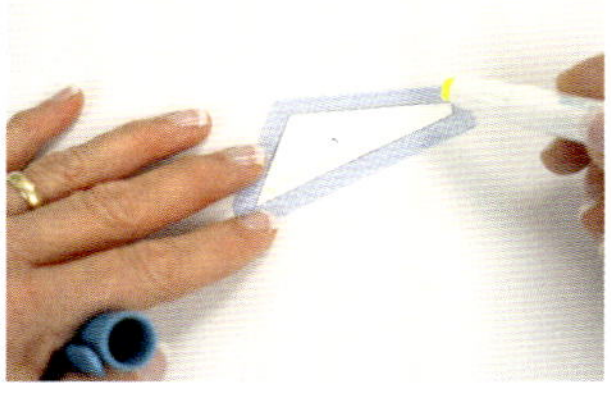

3. Gently fold the seam allowance over the edge of paper and onto the glued area. Do not pull the seam allowances too tightly over the paper.

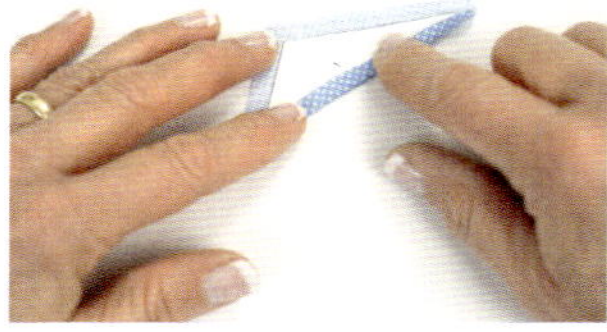

4. As you work around the shape, run glue over the paper and the glued-down seam allowances as needed. Leave the seam allowances at the corners as free as possible.

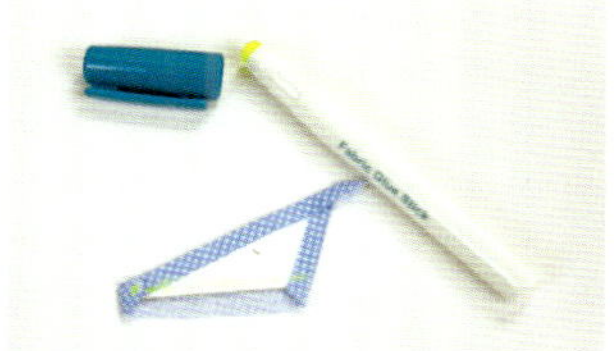

STITCHING

Whipstitch the fabric-covered paper shapes together with strong, fine thread in matching colors and stitches that are close together (see EPP Thread and Sewing Needles, page 6).

Try both the old-school and angled whipstitches (pages 20–21) and use the one that gives you the best results. The angled whipstitch is what I use most often.

Begin Stitching

1. Place 2 adjacent shapes right sides together with the points aligned.

2. Clip the pieces together to hold them in place. Remove the clips when they are no longer needed.

3. Bring your needle through the fabric from back to front at a corner. Bury the knot and thread tail against the paper, under the seam allowance.

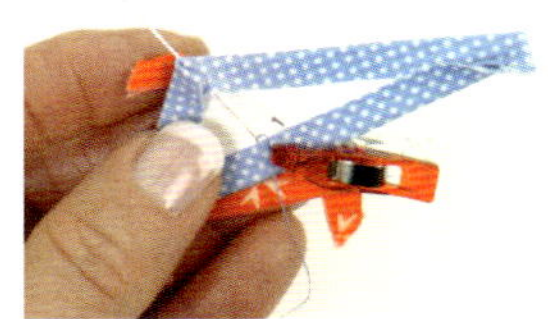

4. Move the corner seam allowances out of your way. Take a stitch through the opposite point and then a second stitch in the same place to anchor the corners in place.

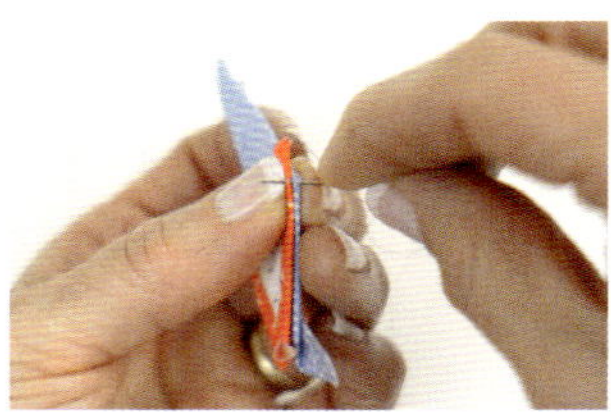

Try not to catch the papers. Catch only as much of the folds of the fabric as you need to hold the fabrics together.

Old-School Whipstitch

In a traditional whipstitch, the needle moves from right to left through the fabric folds at a 90° angle. The thread travels at an angle on the back of your work as you move on to the next stitch.

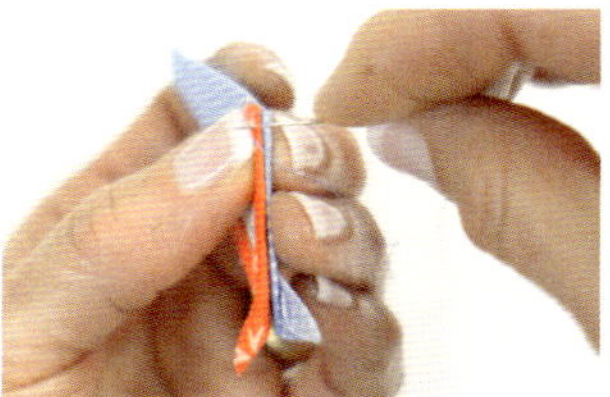

1. Move the needle a small stitch-width away, and take a stitch straight through the folded edge of both fabrics.

2. Pull the thread snugly to seat the stitch and continue in this manner to sew the shapes together.

✱ TIP ✱

How Much Is a Little Bit?

Stitches in EPP are close together, but they can be too close. For me, a little bit is about 1⁄16″, but it varies with the fabric I am sewing. Keep an eye on how your stitches look on both the back and the front, and adjust the distance between them accordingly.

Angled Whipstitch

In an angled whipstitch, the needle travels from right to left at an angle through the fabric. The thread crosses the folds at a 90° angle, and that is what you see on the back of your work.

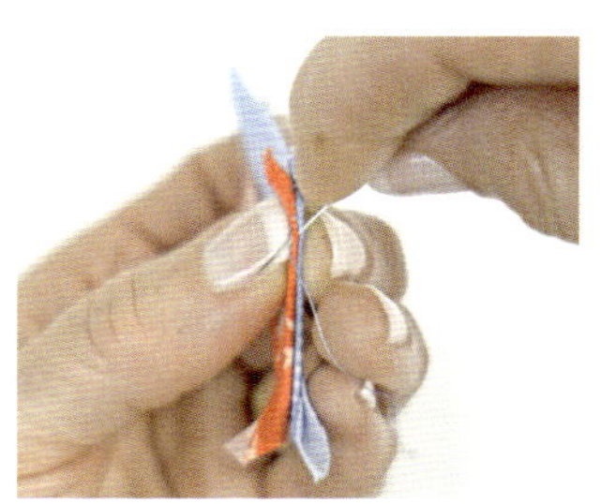

1. Position the point of the needle directly across from the end of the previous stitch. Tilt the needle so it travels at an angle through the folds of the fabric. You should not see the shaft of the needle as it travels through the fabric.

2. Pull the thread snugly to seat the stitch and continue sewing in this manner.

Ending a Line of EPP Stitches

1. Knot (see EPP Ending Knot, page 10) and/or backstitch at the end of the line of stitches.

2. If you will begin sewing the next shape where your line of stitches ends, and if your thread is still strong, continue sewing.

Otherwise, run the needle and thread to the wrong side of the seam allowance, against the paper, and cut the thread, leaving a ¼″ tail.

3. Turn your work over. If your pieces are just a little out of position, that's okay. Pat yourself on the back and be happy!

If the placement is way off, you may need to rip and resew—and then vow to be more careful when you position the next shapes.

NOTE: STITCHING DIRECTIONS

The amount of fabric in your holding hand affects the direction in which you sew.

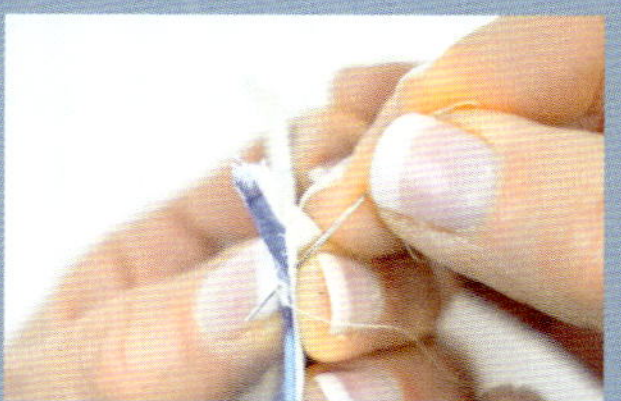

It feels natural to hold small EPP shapes from below, with the edges to be joined at a 90° to your body. That allows you to make the stitch from right to left. The needle enters the fabric from the right and exits to the left.

As units get bigger, you must shift your holding hand to the top of your sewing. It will feel different, but the stitches are basically the same.

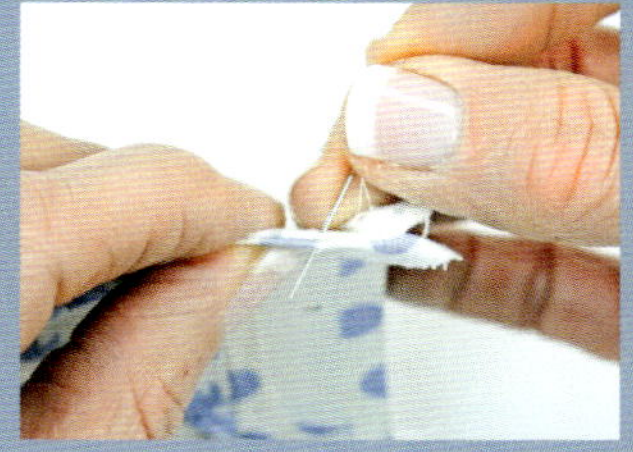

Now the needle enters from the top and exits below the edges of the shapes. The stitch itself does not change.

Some people sew pieces together flat, with shapes resting right side down next to each other on a table or lap board. That does not work well for me, but it may for you.

No matter how you hold your EPP, remember to relax your hands. Stop every now and then and stretch your fingers.

Y-SEAMS

Any time you sew a V-shaped piece into a matching V-shaped opening, you encounter a Y-seam. Y-seams are very common and they are easy to sew.

1. Match one side of the V-shaped piece to the correct side of the V-shaped opening. Begin at the outside points and sew the pieces together. Backstitch at the inner point.

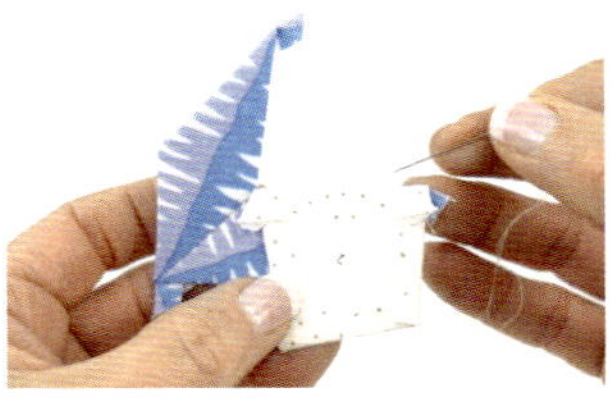

2. Gently move the next side of the V-shaped piece into position. Match the points, bending the papers as needed.

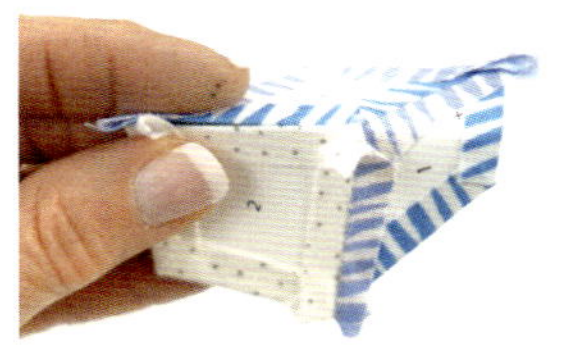

3. Tack stitch (make a stitch over your first stitch) at the beginning of the next line of stitches to lock the points together. Sew the second side of the V-shaped piece in place. It's as simple as that!

CENTER OCTAGONS OR OPTIONAL CIRCLES

Setting in the center octagon on Blocks 1, 6, and 7 requires patience.

Construct the block, leaving an opening for the octagon. The opening will probably be bigger than the octagon. As you sew each side in place, the center comes together.

1. Match one side of the octagon to its corresponding place at the center of the block. Leave the paper inside the octagon, but remove the papers from the directly adjacent shapes only.

Block 1: Remove the paper from shapes 1 and 4.

Block 6: Remove the paper from shapes 1 and 3.

Block 7: Remove the paper from shapes 1 and 2.

2. Sew the 2 edges together from point to point, easing in excess fabric evenly as needed. Move the seam allowances out of your way. Take a backstitch at the point.

3. Remove the papers from the next 2 adjacent shapes, and gently rotate the octagon to bring it into position to sew the next side. Match the points and sew the second side in place.

4. Continue in this manner, removing the papers, rotating the octagon into place, and sewing until the octagon is sewn in place.

Optional Circle Centers

If setting in octagons does not sound like fun, you can appliqué a circle at the center of these (or any) blocks.

1. Remove the papers at the center of the block. Press the seam allowance at the base of these shapes toward the center of the block.

2. Choose any size circle from the Circle Templates (page 46) and use your favorite appliqué technique to complete the center of the block.

3. Very carefully trim away the bulky excess fabric below the circle, leaving a ¼″ seam allowance.

REMOVE THE PAPERS FROM EPP BLOCKS

The papers occupy space, and your blocks will lie flatter once they have been removed. You can remove the papers at the center of each block as you finish them, but *do not* remove the papers that touch the edges of the block yet. If your EPP blocks are going to be sewn to other EPP blocks, it is a lot easier to do if the papers remain in place at the outer edges. That way, they are sewn together the same way the individual pieces go together. If you are going to hand piece the blocks together, or sew them to sashings or borders, you can trace the the outer edge of the paper piece to the wrong side before removing it.

Snip and remove the basting threads; then remove the thread-basted papers. Use an Apliquick Rod or similar pointed tool to gently separate the glued seam allowances from the papers. Try not to fray the raw edges.

PRESSING EPP BLOCKS

Gently press the blocks from the back. Steam can help to flatten and shape the blocks.

Pay attention to the seam allowances in EPP blocks, and only change their direction if it makes sense to do so.

EPP BLOCK SIZE

Don't be surprised if your blocks do not have a finished size of 8″ × 8″. My own blocks averaged 8⅛″ × 8⅛″. Why are they bigger?

* Fabric folded over the paper adds to the size of the shape. Some, but not all, of the fabric gets taken up in the seam. The more pieces in a block, the bigger the impact will be.
* Fabric thickness impacts the finished size of the block.
* There are 8 different EPP block designs which leads to variations in their finished sizes.

Happily, there is more leeway in hand sewing when it comes to making shapes fit together. With blocks that are ⅛″–¼″ apart in size, you can ease in the excess fabric without it being too obvious. More than that and you will need to trim a big block or add coping strips to a small block.

PRACTICE WITH HEXAGONS

Hexagons are a great starting point for English paper-piecing (EPP). The sturdy paper templates make it easy to sew their short seams together. Try one of these hexagon templates to practice your skills, or dive into the more intricate EPP blocks on the next pages. And remember, EPP isn't just for hexagons—you can use it with all sorts of shapes!

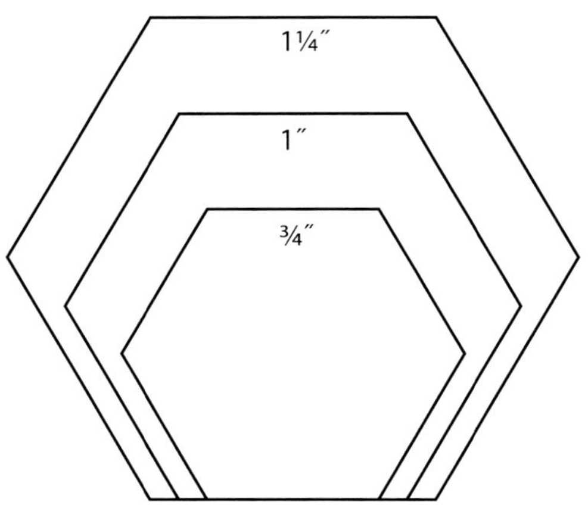

THE BLOCKS

Refer to the English Paper-Piecing Techniques (page 12) for all blocks.

I strongly recommend that you set aside the uncut block-corner papers until most of the quilt blocks are complete. They are an accent that can be used to unify the appearance of a quilt as a whole.

Remember that you can combine small contiguous shapes into larger shapes in any block where it makes sense for you to do so. See Tip: You Are in Control (page 14).

You can play around with color placement for the blocks using the Coloring Pages (page 58–62).

BLOCK 1

1. Refer to the block diagram on page 31 and arrange the shapes as shown, with the printed side of the papers facing you.

2. Sew the 1-2-3 and 4-5-6 shapes together into units.

3. Look closely at the block diagram and place a 1-2-3 unit next to a 4-5-6 unit. Be sure the bottom edges of shapes 1 and 4 form a straight line. Sew the units together to make 8 pairs.

4. Sew the pairs from Step 3 together into quadrants. Sew the quadrants together; then sew the 2 sides of the block together.

5. Set-in the center octagon (see Center Octagons or Optional Circles, page 25), or appliqué a circle at the block center.

6. Set aside corners 8-9-10.

Patterns on page 47.

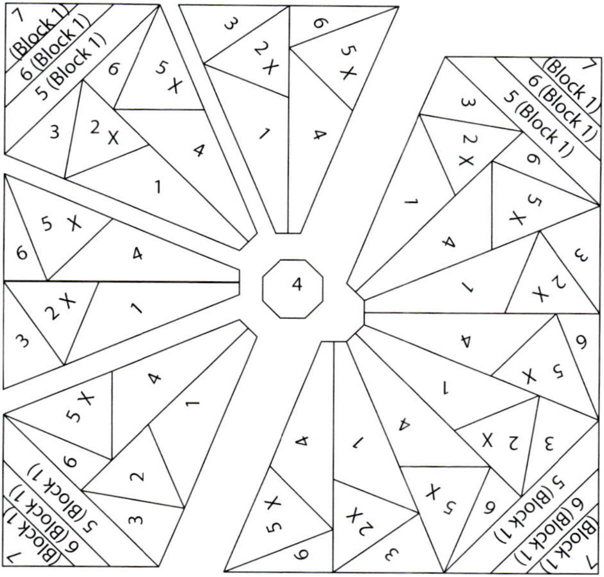

✳ TIP ✳

Ignore the Seam Allowances at the Points

Flip the excess fabric at the points out of your way. Concentrate on the straight edges as you sew from point to point.

BLOCK 2

1. Refer to the block diagram. Arrange the shapes with the printed side of the papers facing you.

2. Place 2 diamonds 1 side by side with the X's at the center of the block. Sew them together into pairs.

3. Sew a diamond 2 in place to make 4 of the 1-1-2 units. See Y-Seams (page 24).

4. Sew the units from Step 3 together to form a star.

5. Sew the remaining diamonds 2 in place.

6. Sew the diamonds 3 in place.

7. Sew the diamonds 4 in place.

8. Set aside corners 5-6-7.

Patterns on page 48.

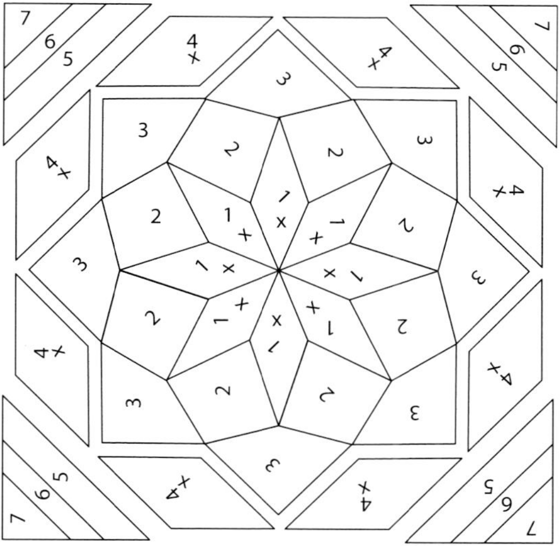

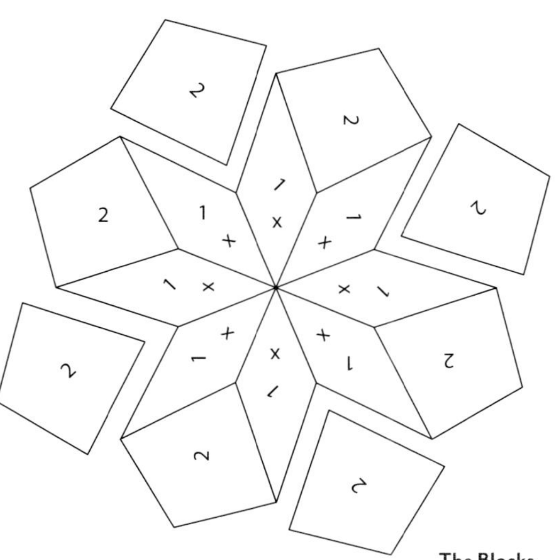

BLOCK 3

1. Refer to the block diagram. Arrange the shapes as shown, with the printed side of the papers facing you.

2. Sew the 1-2-3 shapes together into units.

3. Sew the units from Step 2 together in pairs, then quadrants, and then sew the 2 sides of the block together.

4. Set aside corners 4-5-6.

Patterns on page 49.

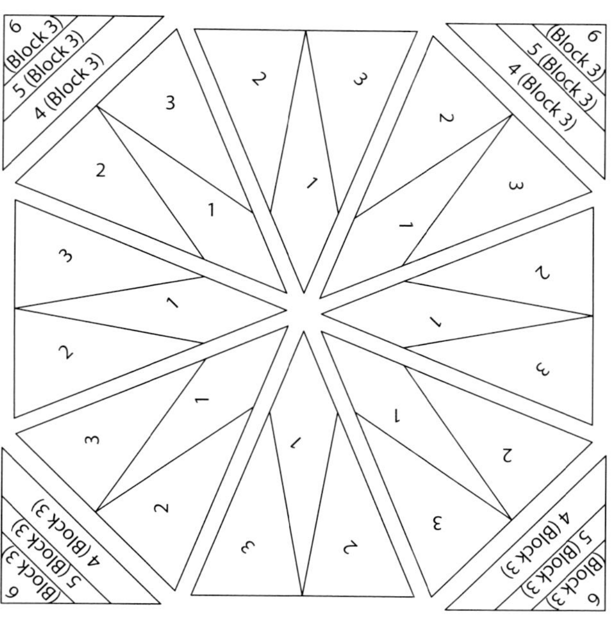
6
(Block 3)
5 (Block 3)
4 (Block 3)
3
2
1
2
3
1
2
1
3
6
(Block 3)
5 (Block 3)
4 (Block 3)
3
1
2
1
2
3
1
3
2
1
2
3
1
3
2
4 (Block 3)
5 (Block 3)
(Block 3)
6
4 (Block 3)
5 (Block 3)
(Block 3)
6

BLOCK 4

This block has many sharp points. Here are some tips for dealing with them:

* Take your time.
* As you sew, hold the fabric over the papers with more force so you can get to the true edges by the paper.
* Even though the shapes are small, do not cut your seam allowance too short, as it may fray. Trim as needed after the papers have been removed.
* When pressing, "swirl" the seam allowances around the points on the back side of the block. Use a pointed tool to manipulate the fabric to reduce fraying.
* Feel free to appliqué a circle over the bulky intersection where the points meet (page 25).

1. Refer to the block diagram. Arrange the shapes as shown, with the printed side of the papers facing you.

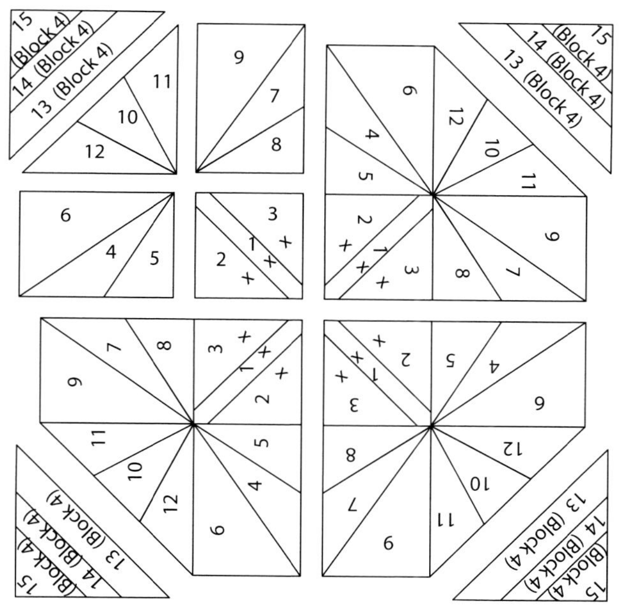

2. Sew the 1-2-3, 4-5-6, 7-8-9, and 10-11-12 shapes together into units.

3. Sew the units from Step 2 together into 4 quadrants.

4. Sew the quadrants together into pairs; then sew the pairs together.

5. Set aside corners 13-14-15.

Patterns on pages 50–51.

BLOCK 5

Shapes 4, 5, 6, and 7 can be cut apart to make 4 or fewer strips. You could leave the wedge intact and cover it with a single fabric. The choice is yours.

1. Refer to the block diagram. Arrange the shapes as shown, with the printed side of the papers facing you.

2. Sew the 1-2-3 and the 4-5-6-7 shapes together into units.

3. Sew the units from Step 2 together in pairs, then quadrants, and then sew the 2 sides of the block together.

4. Set aside corners 8-9-10.

Patterns on pages 51–52.

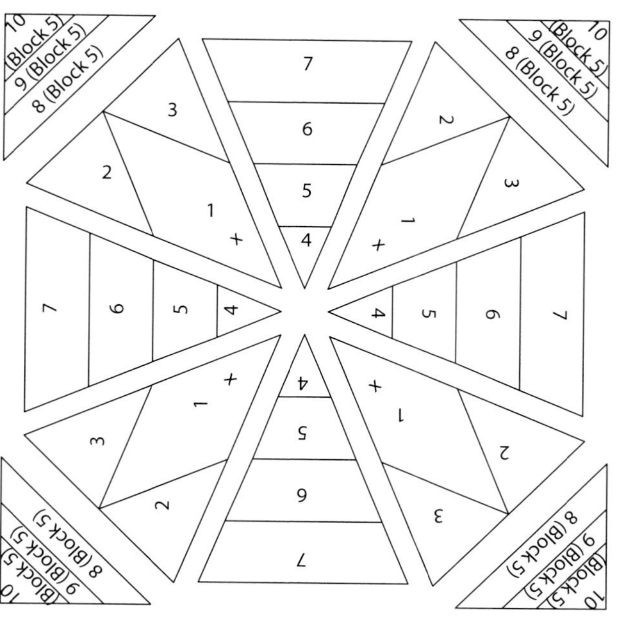
10 (Block 5)
9 (Block 5)
8 (Block 5)
7
6
5
4
3
2
1
x

BLOCK 6

1. Refer to the block diagram. Arrange the shapes as shown, with the printed side of the papers facing you.

2. Sew the 1-2 and 3-4 shapes together into units.

3. Sew the 1-2 units to the 3-4 units, leaving a V-shaped opening for triangle 5.

4. Position and sew a triangle 5 in place. See Y-Seams (page 24). Repeat for all units.

5. Sew the units together in pairs, then quadrants, and then sew the 2 sides of the block together.

6. Set-in hexagon 6 or appliqué a circle at the block center.

7. Set aside corners 7-8-9.

Patterns on page 53.

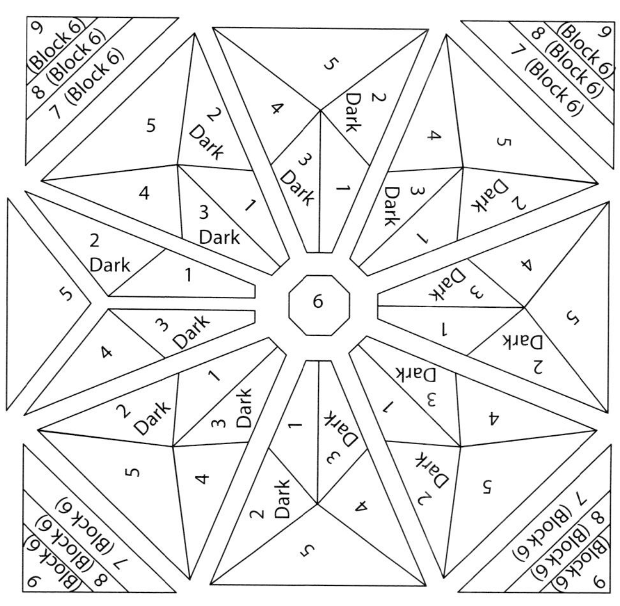
9 (Block 6) 8 (Block 6) 7 (Block 6)
5 2 Dark 4 3 Dark 1
5 4 2 Dark 3 Dark 1
4 5 3 Dark 2 Dark 1
9 (Block 6) 8 (Block 6) 7 (Block 6)
2 Dark 1 5 3 Dark 4
6
4 3 Dark 1 5 2 Dark
2 Dark 1 3 Dark 5 4
3 Dark 1 4 2 Dark 5
1 3 Dark 2 Dark 4 5
9 (Block 6) 8 (Block 6) 7 (Block 6)
7 (Block 6) 8 (Block 6) 9 (Block 6)

BLOCK 7

I combined shapes 3 and 4 into 1 piece. You can cut them apart, or not—the choice is yours.

1. Refer to the block diagram. Arrange the shapes as shown, with the printed side of the papers facing you.

2. Sew the 1-2 shapes together, being sure the bottom edges form a straight line.

3. Sew the 3-4 shapes together.

4. Sew the 1-2 units to the 3-4 units.

5. Sew the 5-6-7 triangles together into units.

6. Position and sew the 1-2-3-4 units to the 5-6-7 units.

7. Sew the units together in pairs, then quadrants, and then sew the 2 sides of the block together.

8. Set aside corners 8-9-10.

Patterns on page 54.

BLOCK 8

1. Refer to the block diagram. Arrange the shapes as shown, with the printed side of the papers facing you.

2. Sew the 1-1-2 shapes together.

3. Sew the 1-1-2 units together to form the block center. Sew the diamonds 3 in place.

4. Sew the 4-5-6 shapes together. The shapes are small, but you can do it!

5. Sew the 4-5-6 units to the triangle 7.

6. Sew 4-5-6-7 units in place.

7. Set aside corners 8-9-10.

Patterns on page 55–56.

10 (Block 8)
9 (Block 8)
8 (Block 8)
1x
2
3
4
5
6
7x

1x
2
3

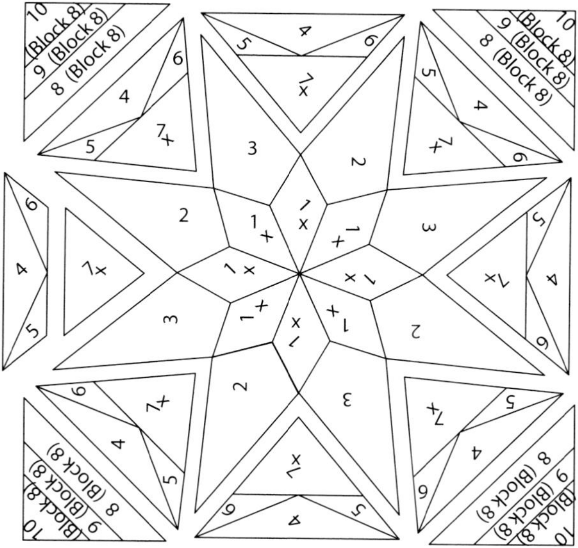

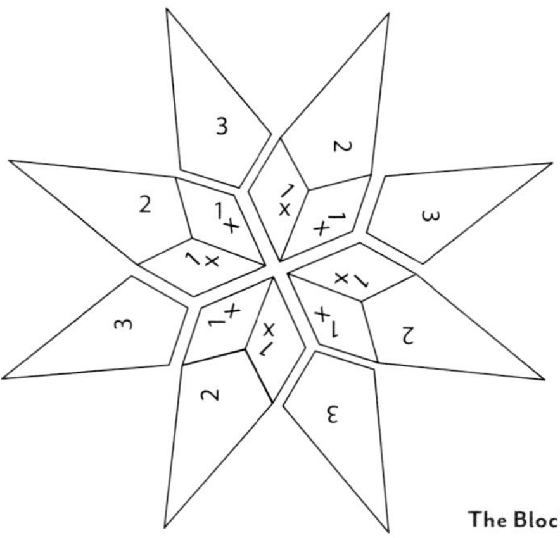

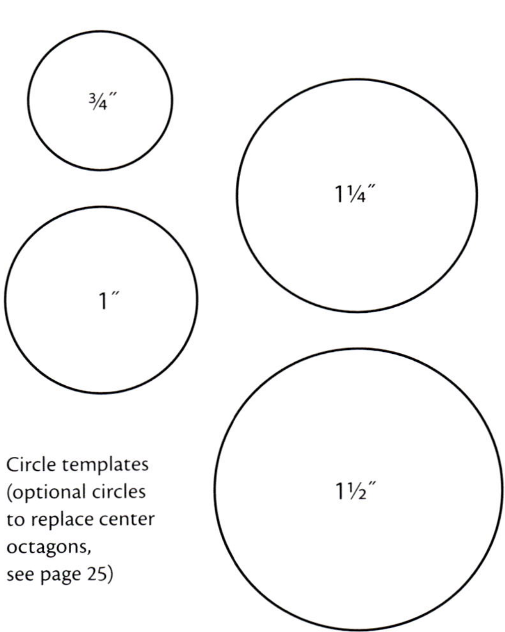

Circle templates (optional circles to replace center octagons, see page 25)

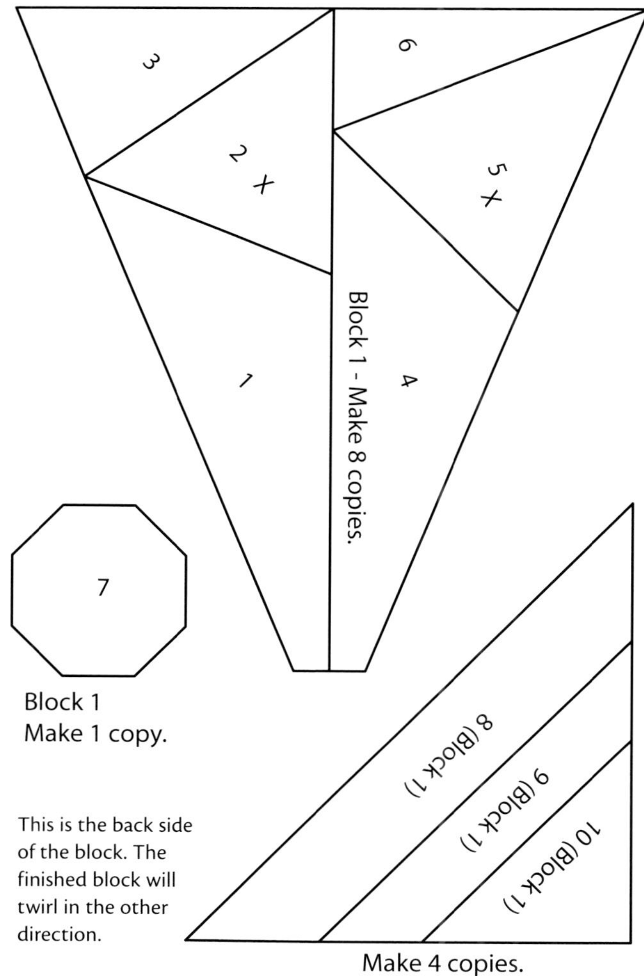

Block 1
Make 1 copy.

This is the back side of the block. The finished block will twirl in the other direction.

Make 4 copies.

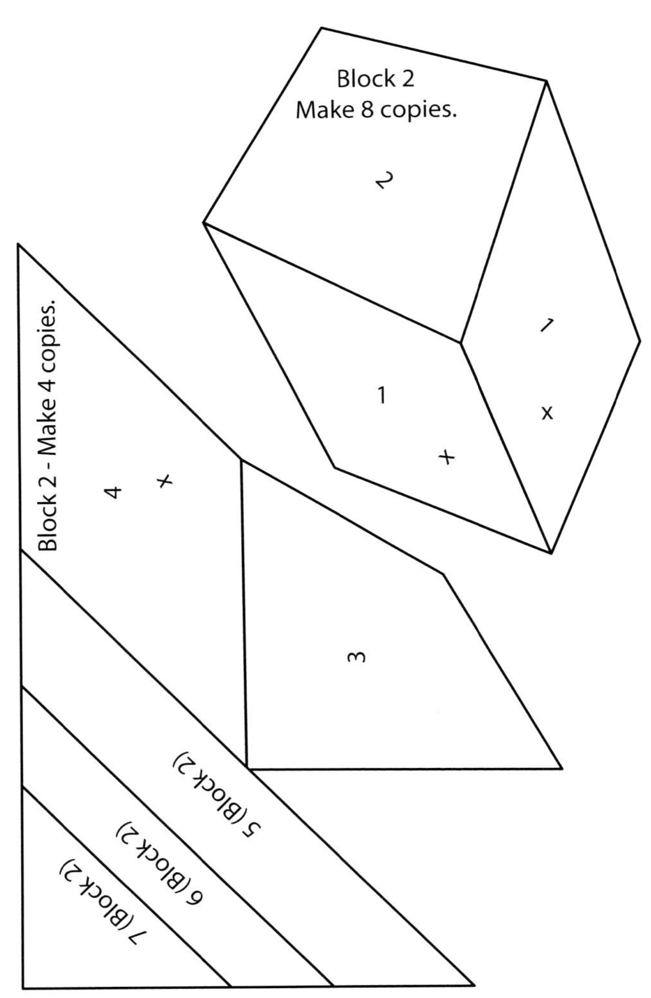
Block 2
Make 8 copies.
2
1
1
x
x
Block 2 - Make 4 copies.
4
x
3
5 (Block 2)
6 (Block 2)
7 (Block 2)

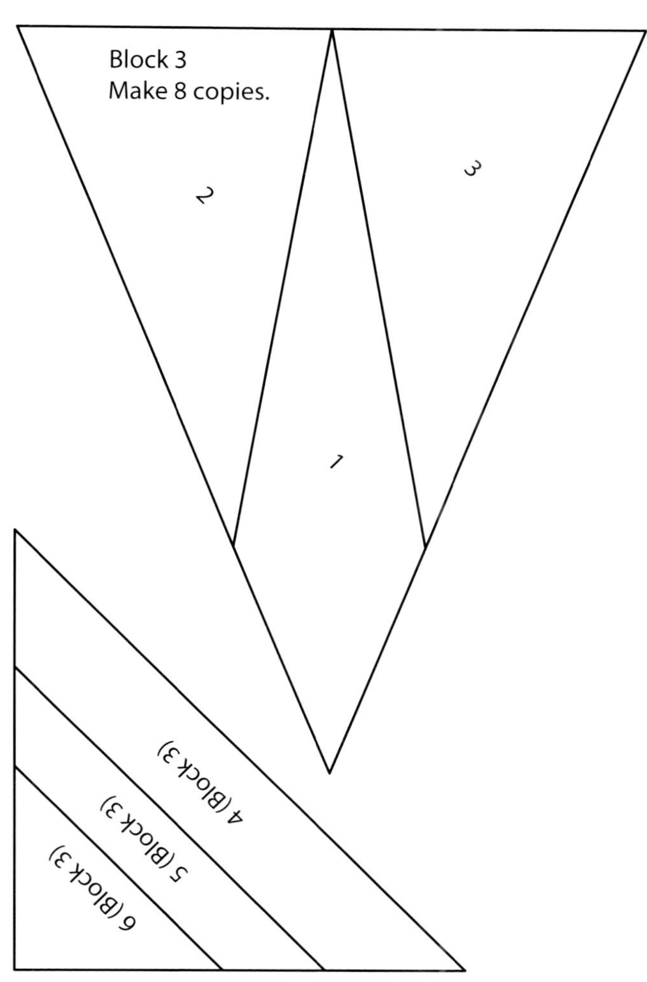
Block 3
Make 8 copies.
2
3
1
4 (Block 3)
5 (Block 3)
6 (Block 3)
Make 4 copies.

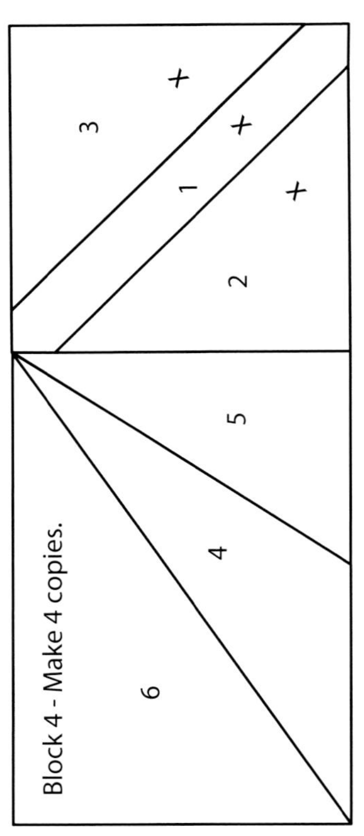
Block 4 - Make 4 copies.
1
2
3
4
5
6

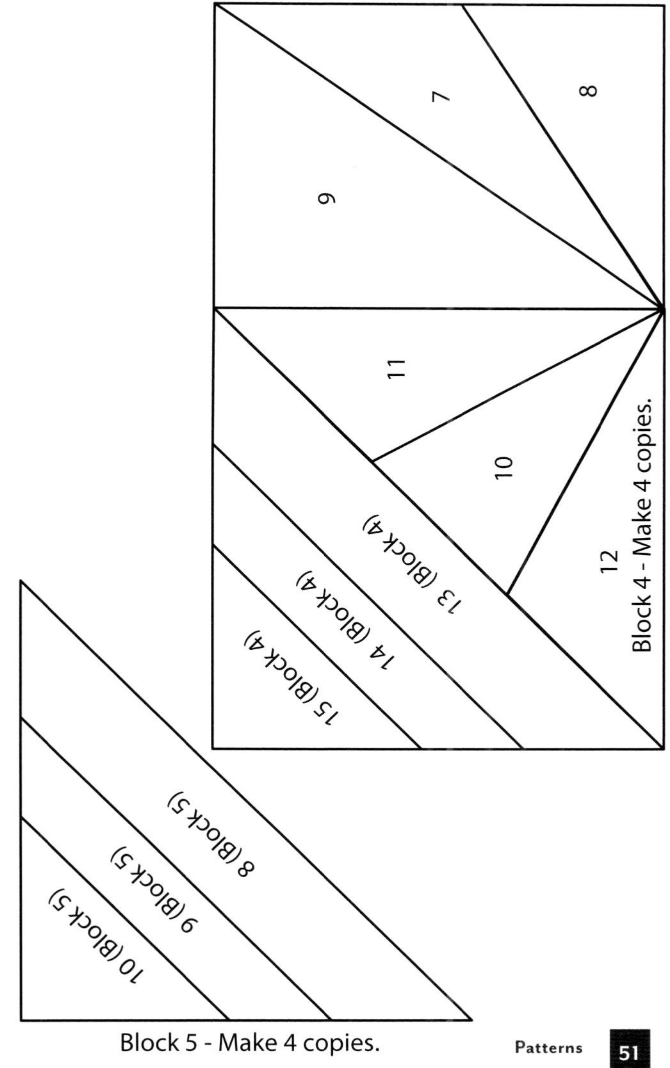

Block 4 - Make 4 copies.

Block 5 - Make 4 copies.

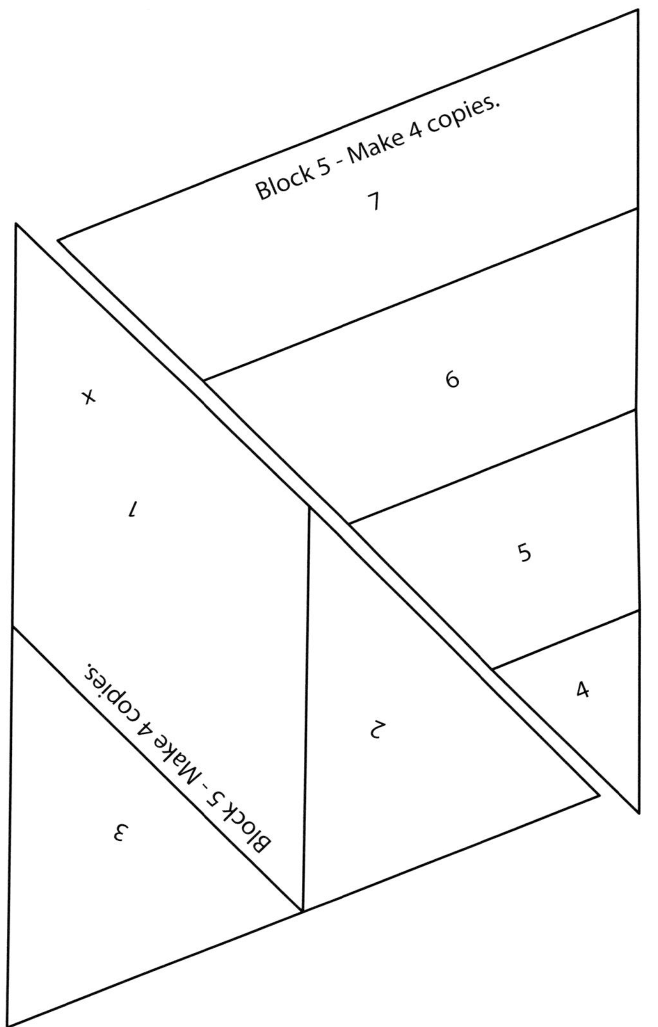
Block 5 - Make 4 copies.
7
6
5
4
x
1
2
3
Block 5 - Make 4 copies.

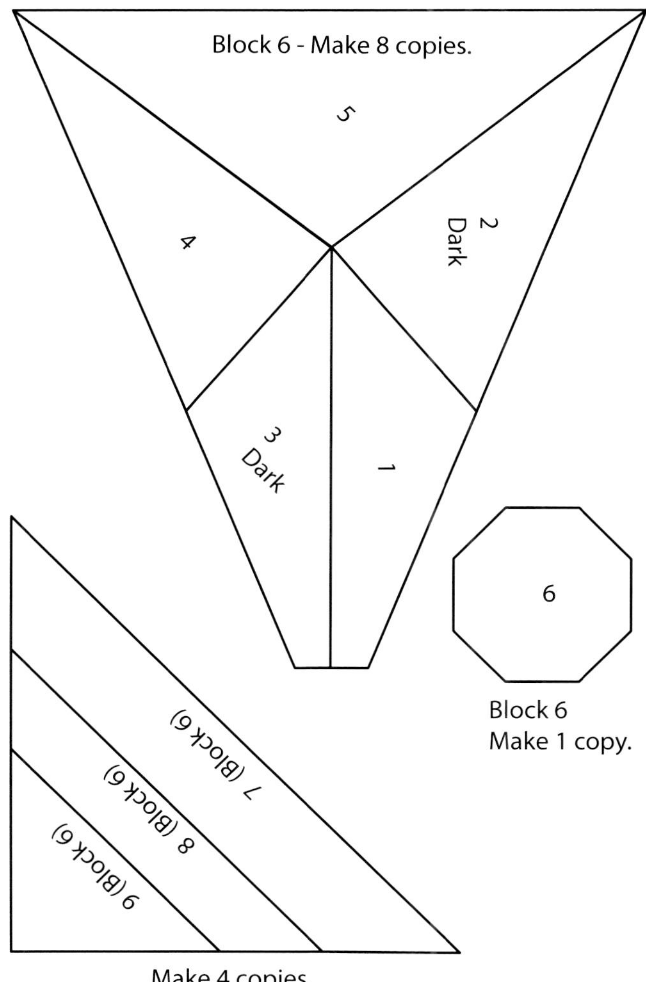

Block 6
Make 1 copy.

Make 4 copies.

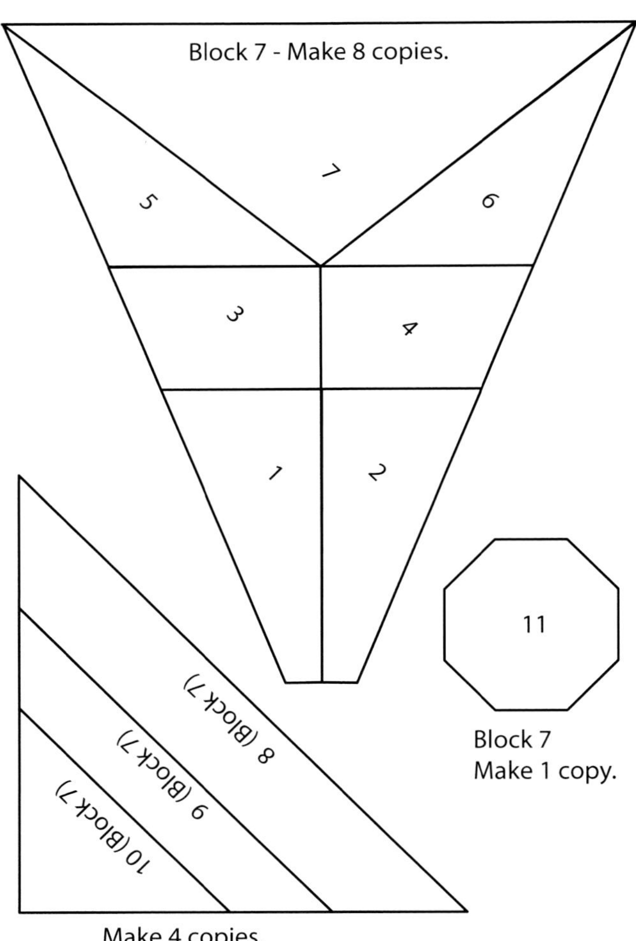

Block 7
Make 1 copy.

Make 4 copies.

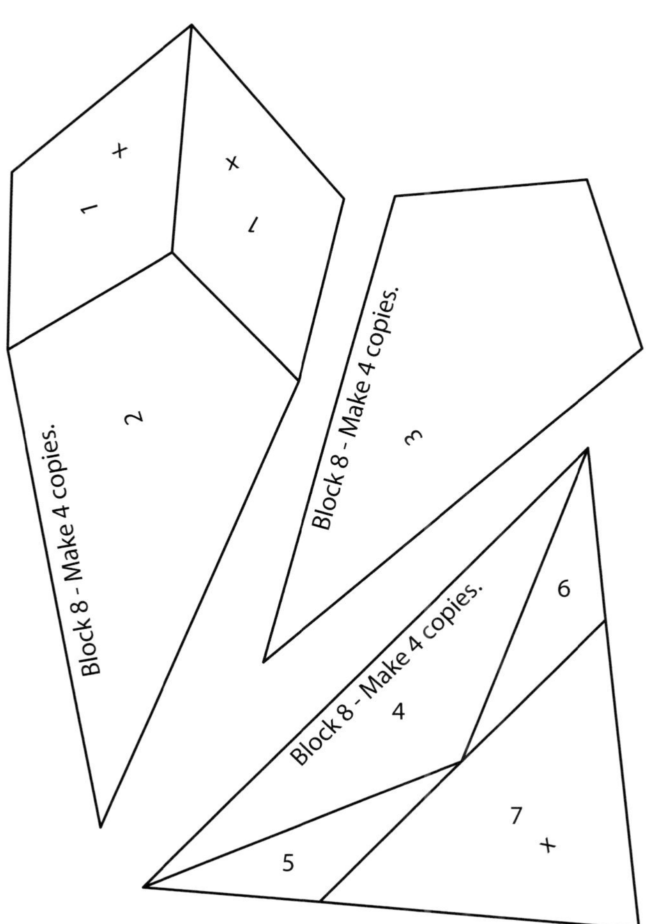
Block 8 - Make 4 copies.
1
2
Block 8 - Make 4 copies.
3
Block 8 - Make 4 copies.
4
5
6
7

Make 4 copies.

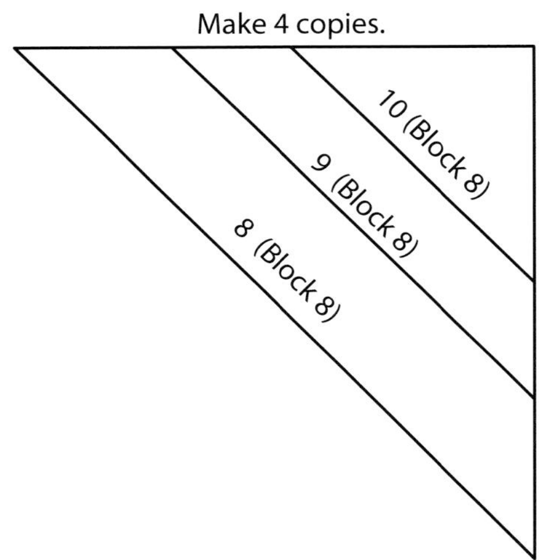

COLORING PAGES

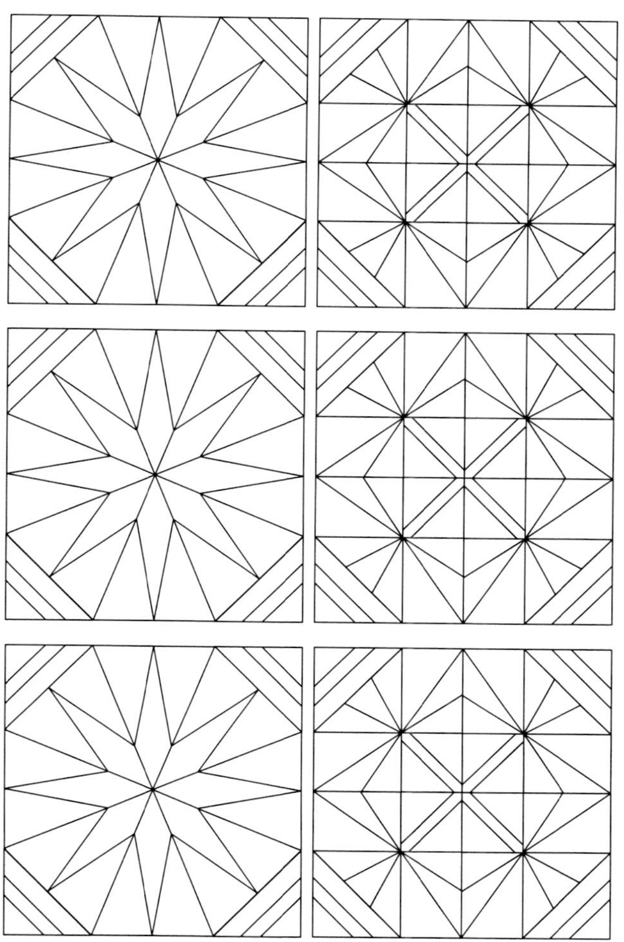

Publisher: Amy Barrett-Daffin

Creative Director: Gailen Runge

Senior Editor: Roxane Cerda

Editors: Liz Aneloski and Gailen Runge

Technical Editor: Debbie Rodgers

Cover/Book Designer: April Mostek

Production Coordinator: Tim Manibusan

Illustrator: Becky Goldsmith

Photography Coordinator: Rachel Ackley

Photography by Becky Goldsmith, unless otherwise noted

Published by C&T Publishing, Inc., P.O. Box 1456, Lafayette, CA 94549

Printed in the USA

10 9 8 7 6 5 4 3 2

ABOUT THE AUTHOR

Becky Goldsmith grew up in Oklahoma and met her wonderful husband, Steve, at the University of Oklahoma. They married in 1978, at the end of their senior year, and they are still happy together. They do their best to support each other in all of their endeavors.

In addition to her creative work, Becky wears many hats—she's a wife, mom, grandmother, and even a certified yoga instructor, always striving for balance, strength, and joy in everything she does.

Designing and making quilts and teaching others how to make quilts is a better career than Becky could ever have imagined. Quilters are wonderful people, and she loves being a part of the global quilt world. Becky would like to thank you for including her in your quilting life!

Visit Becky online and follow on social media!
Website: pieceocake.com
Facebook: /beckygoldsmith.pieceocake
Instagram: @beckygoldsmith
YouTube: /beckygoldsmith